Healthy Foods around the World

by Beth Bence Reinke, MS, RD

BUMBA BOOKS™

LERNER PUBLICATIONS ◆ MINNEAPOLIS

Note to Educators:

Throughout this book, you'll find critical thinking questions. These can be used to engage young readers in thinking critically about the topic and in using the text and photos to do so.

Lerner Publications Company
A division of Lerner Publishing Group, Inc.
241 First Avenue North
Minneapolis, MN 55401 USA

For reading levels and more information, look up this title at www.lernerbooks.com.

Library of Congress Cataloging-in-Publication Data

Names: Reinke, Beth Bence, author.
Title: Healthy foods around the world / Beth Bence Reinke, MS, RD.
Description: Minneapolis : Lerner Publications, [2018] | Series: Bumba books. Nutrition matters | Audience: Ages 4–7. | Audience: K to grade 3. | Includes bibliographical references and index.
Identifiers: LCCN 2017058942 (print) | LCCN 2017047871 (ebook) | ISBN 9781541507685 (eb pdf) | ISBN 9781541503410 (lb : alk. paper) | ISBN 9781541526815 (pb : alk. paper)
Subjects: LCSH: Food habits—Juvenile literature. | International cooking—Juvenile literature. | Nutrition—Juvenile literature.
Classification: LCC GT2850 (print) | LCC GT2850 .R4525 2018 (ebook) | DDC 394.1/2—dc23

LC record available at https://lccn.loc.gov/2017058942

Manufactured in the United States of America
1 – CG – 7/15/18

Table of Contents

Tour Time!

Let's take a tour of

healthy foods.

Kids around the world

eat healthy foods.

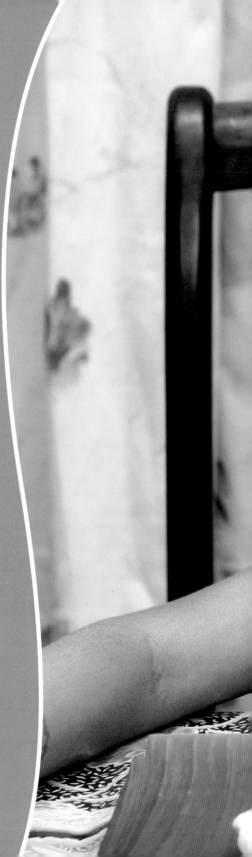

Kids in Spain eat gazpacho.

It is cold vegetable soup.

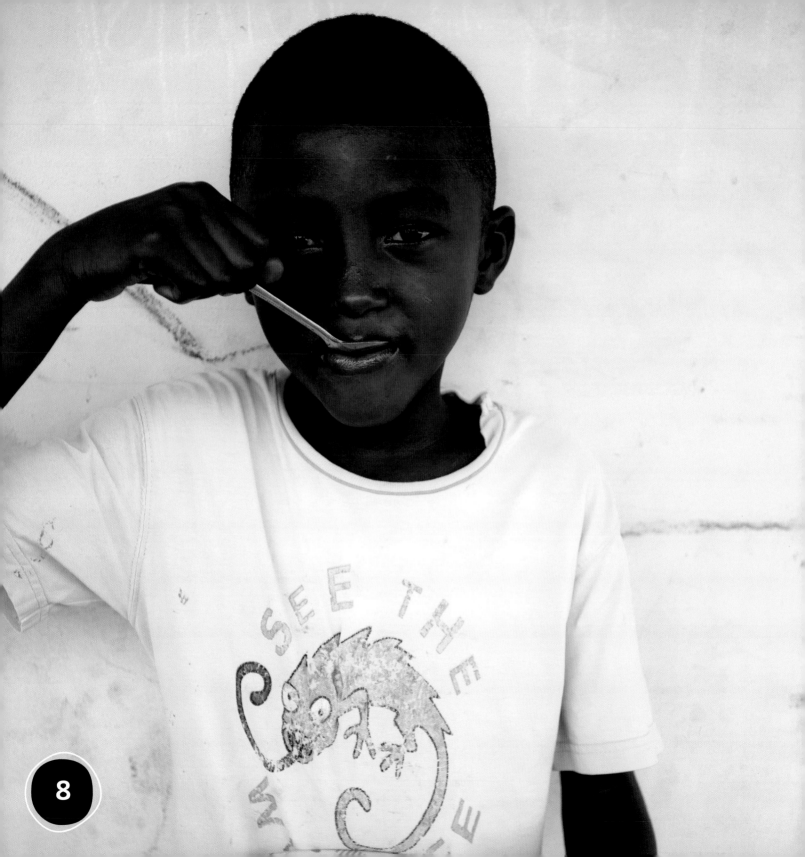

In Ghana, kids eat fufu.

Fufu is mashed yams.

People in Japan eat healthy foods

from the sea.

They eat fish and seaweed.

Can you guess why seafood might be common in Japan?

Many families in Mexico like

hot peppers.

Cooks mix them into rice.

In Australia, kids enjoy Vegemite.

It is a spread with vitamin B.

People in India eat lentils with spices.

They also eat raita, a kind of yogurt.

In Brazil, kids eat cassava.

It looks a little like a potato.

Cassava is a vegetable. Can you name other healthy vegetables?

People eat different foods

in different places.

But everyone likes tasty,

healthy food!

World Map

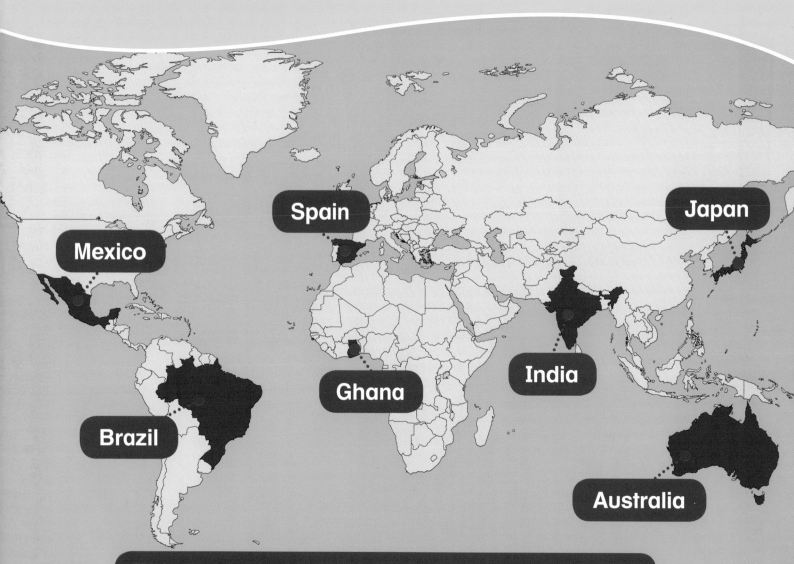

Spain

Japan

Mexico

India

Ghana

Brazil

Australia

This map shows where each country in this book can be found.

Picture Glossary

lentils

flat, round seeds related to peas and beans

tour

a trip to learn and explore

Vegemite

a food spread made from yeast

yams

white root vegetables that grow in Africa

23

Read More

Boothroyd, Jennifer. *Taste Something New! Giving Different Foods a Try.* Minneapolis: Lerner Publications, 2016.

Bullard, Lisa. *My Food, Your Food.* Minneapolis: Millbrook Press, 2015.

Meister, Cari. *Meals in India.* Minneapolis: Bullfrog Books, 2017.

Index

Photo Credits